Sing a Rainbow

Musical activities
with
mentally handicapped children

DAVID WARD

London
OXFORD UNIVERSITY PRESS
New York Melbourne
1979

Oxford University Press, Walton Street, Oxford OX2 6DP

OXFORD   LONDON   GLASGOW   NEW YORK
TORONTO   MELBOURNE   WELLINGTON   CAPE TOWN
IBADAN   NAIROBI   DAR ES SALAAM
KUALA LUMPUR   SINGAPORE   JAKARTA   HONG KONG   TOKYO
DELHI   BOMBAY   CALCUTTA   MADRAS   KARACHI

First published 1979
ISBN 0 19 317416 2

By the same author
Hearts and Hands and Voices

Acknowledgements

We are grateful to the following for permission to reproduce copyright material:

James Blades for words to 'Big Ben' tune; Chappell & Co. Ltd for 'Sing a Rainbow' from
film *Pete Kelly's Blues*, words and music by Arthur Hamilton © 1955 Mark VII Music by
kind permission of Chappell Morris Ltd and Mark VII Ltd; EMI Music Publishing Ltd,
138–140 Charing Cross Road, London WC2H 0LD for 'Horsey! Horsey!' © 1937 Francis
Day & Hunter Ltd.

Permission to use 'Sing a Rainbow' for title of the book also kindly granted by Chappell
Morris Ltd.

The cover photograph is reproduced by kind permission of the National Society for
Mentally Handicapped Children.

Printed and bound in Great Britain at
The Camelot Press Ltd, Southampton

Contents

Foreword

In the last ten years or so there has been a great improvement in the provision of education for mentally handicapped children. April 1971 saw the implementation of State education for *all* children in the United Kingdom, thus bringing in a considerable number of handicapped children who, up to that date, had been officially thought unsuitable for education in schools.

This provision was long overdue. Many parents and educationists had pressed for schooling for these children, sometimes with the mistaken idea that this would, by concentrating on reading, writing, and numeracy, be a good step towards normality.

Experience has shown, however, that many mentally handicapped children respond surprisingly well to a rich variety of activities such as one would find in a lively nursery school. Music occupies an important position amongst these activities because through enjoyable participation in it, children learn to manipulate language, to listen, to co-ordinate mind and body, and to become aware of the things around them.

The activities suggested in this book are based on the author's extensive and regular experience as a teacher of handicapped children. All the material has been well tried with various groups in special schools, and most of the approaches are easily initiated by teachers with only modest musical skills.

A book, however, can only present the appropriate material and describe the processes by which it is applied. There is always the very important additional factor – the teacher or therapist – who must bring it all to life by his or her enthusiasm and sensitivity. However simple the activities, what matters most is the quality of the experience of these activities.

Music is probably the best medium which can exploit sensitive communication – a basic need of all humans.

David Ward

1 The activities

Responses to sounds can be observed in human babies as early as the second week of life. These responses usually take the form of generalized movements towards the sources of the sounds. At the same age, babies will display the fascinating 'startle' reflex movement when loud sounds are made near to them.

Domestic animals respond appropriately to human vocal inflexions; they tend to cower when we speak gruffly to them, and to show pleasure when we adopt a coaxing tone. Dogs often produce a strange howling sound when mouth-organs or other reed instruments are played near to them, and horses demonstrate clear signs of excitement when they are on parade with an accompanying brass band. Most animals use their 'voices' to express intense fear, pain or aggression; cats in particular have a well-known method of expressing pleasure – i.e. by purring when we fondle and feed them.

Animals and humans seem to respond instinctively to environmental sounds; sounds also enable them to express certain feelings. Musical sounds, which largely belong to human experience, similarly evoke instinctive responses and serve as a means of expressing feelings.

These two aspects of musical activity – i.e. active listening and performing – need to be considered when sessions are initiated with mentally handicapped children. Sometimes our aim might be to provoke a movement of the head or eyes by making interesting sounds near a child; on other occasions we might try to get him to generate his own vocal, bodily or instrumental sounds.

It is important to understand what we mean by 'response'. Student teachers (and some parents) often report that their handicapped children 'respond well' to music. This is often a vague and generalized observation which is perhaps well-meaning but over-generous.

Teachers and therapists who work with handicapped children need to acquire knowledge about the ways in which very young *normal* children respond to musical sounds; it is also necessary to know how the first musical sounds are normally produced. This knowledge can then be related and applied to the activities of handicapped children.

When we say that a child responds well we need to know how the particular response relates to normal levels of development. Thus, a ten-year-old child whose general developmental level is comparable with that of a normal five-year-old should not surprise us when he 'dances' (i.e. bounces rhythmically) to a lively tune. On the other hand, a seriously handicapped child who functions at the six-month level deserves great praise for demonstrating the same rhythmic response.

Most teachers of handicapped children are familiar with the concept of developmental levels. This concept affords a more optimistic approach to activities with handicapped children. The terms *mental deficiency, occupation,* and *care* have given way to *handicap* and *education.* A developmental approach makes intelligent use of the information we have about normal children. By relating the functioning of our handicapped children to normal developmental levels we are able to devise activities appropriate for them and plan progressive activities in our programmes of work.

It is, of course, essential to break down progressive steps as finely as possible for our most severely handicapped pupils; normal children sometimes pass through certain stages so quickly that we do not notice that they have done so. We need also to remember that very few of our handicapped children fall neatly into a developmental niche. They are notoriously uneven in various aspects of development, and we must make careful assessments of their physical, emotional and intellectual levels whenever we devise activities or present material for them.

How does music fit into a developmental scheme and why is it an especially valuable educational medium?

At the earliest stage handicapped children need frequent and varied activities based especially on the sound/response idea. It is vitally important to educate children at all levels through the *aural sense* and children who are at this sound/response stage have an especial need for appropriate activity. The problem for the teacher is to find enough different and interesting activities to fully engage the children at this level. This book attempts to describe some of the activities which have been found to be successful for mentally handicapped children at 'special care'[1] and later stages of development.

A number of studies[2] have been carried out to attempt to ascertain how music is perceived. The results of these studies have often been very dependent upon intellectual responses, and because of this we have little knowledge of the way in which children who cannot rationalize their responses actually perceive sounds. The observations of music teachers and therapists suggest that musical perception is a complex process involving much more than conscious activity. We know that music can sometimes trigger off associations and deeply rooted emotions. Strongly rhythmic music may affect us physically, without necessarily involving conscious thought. Our experience of music involves much more than our ears and brains. Thus, in presenting musical activities to young children we need to use approaches which involve movement, vision and touch. Not only do these approaches help to ensure that the children are fully involved, but they also allow for certain sensory deficiencies which often occur in mentally handicapped children and which inevitably add to their learning problems.

It is impossible to provide a detailed programme or scheme of work for the entire range of age and ability of severely handicapped children in the special school. Activities may be directed towards individuals and groups of varying sizes, and,

---

[1] At the time of writing it is common practice in English special schools to form small groups of the most severely handicapped children and to call them 'special care' children. Other children in the special schools tend to be grouped in small classes roughly according to age and level of maturity.

[2] See *The Psychology of Music* by Rosamund Shuter, published by Methuen.

because there are such wide individual differences in these children, one can only hope for a skeleton scheme to give a general guide to overall progress in their musical and educational development. The following table of stages attempts to show this progression:

1. Physical responses to sound. These tend to move from generalized to specific responses.
2. Vocalized and other bodily sounds produced by the children to express basic emotions – e.g. joy, peacefulness.
3. The discrimination of sounds.
4. Vocal sounds produced by the children to express increasingly specific and complex feelings and meanings.
5. Precise physical actions which may be taught or produced as a result of exploration and improvisation.
6. The understanding of a wide variety of information, both musical and that which is associated with musical activity.
7. Creative activity.

These stages (from 1 to 7) are not strictly progressive. For example, children may begin *creating* vocal sounds at stage 2; physical responses (stage 1) may later be very sophisticated and finely expressive in dance and movement. In other words, progress can be traced both through stages 1 to 7 and also *within each stage*. A music session might include the following ingredients which relate to any of these stages: something to look at, something to listen to, something to hold or touch, something definite to do, something to invent, something to imagine, something to make a decision about, something to move to.

By appealing to as many senses as possible, we may be successful in finding at least one *strength* – e.g. a child may be especially attracted by the appearance of an instrument, or by the movements which are employed by its player.

A multi-sensory approach is recommended, not only because the children will probably have sensory handicaps, but also because some may have sensory strengths. We are more likely to succeed by building on what the children can do, rather than attempting to remedy a severe weakness.

Music to engage and extend the children's attention

The most seriously handicapped children – i.e. those in the special care class – need appropriate stimulation of the aural and other senses. This is a basic requirement which, if met makes progress in several directions possible. For these particular children, an individual approach is vital, but this need not be restricted to the system in which the teacher withdraws the children one by one from the classroom. There is much to be gained by having them grouped in a semi-circular formation in much the same way as for more able groups. Some children seem to sense that something special is going to happen when they are put into their places, the classroom aides and other therapists enjoy the supportive roles they are expected to play, and the level of noise is often reduced. It may, of course be necessary to arrange to withdraw those children whose uncontrolled noises make it impossible to work at all; in the author's opinion this is justifiable if it ensures that, at least for the duration of the music session, the majority of the children are able to get maximum benefit.

Select a brightly coloured maraca which makes a strong sound. Try to suggest the idea that the instrument has a 'personality' by saying 'he is coming to see you!' and approach the children individually, sounding 'him' quite near to their faces. For most of them, the sound needs to be made gently and carefully at first to avoid fear or anxiety; a few children will need a firm, strong approach involving the use of louder sounds. Some children are prone to an overspill of energy and seem to 'over-respond'; these need to be approached very tentatively. Explore various ways of producing the sound, sometimes making a short but continuous swishing sound, sometimes playing rhythmic motifs, e.g.

Observe the children the whole time, especially noting whether they blink their eyes or change their facial expressions or move in any way in response to the sounds. Repeat the stimulus, now changing the *point where the sound is made,* perhaps by each ear, over the head, behind the head, directly in front of the eyes. Certain children may not respond in spite of repeated sounds from this instrument; for these, a different instrument must be tried later.

For those who do respond in any way whatsoever, here is the beginning of a surprisingly large variety of activities based on this simple idea – i.e. the use of a sound to provoke physical or emotional responses. If more than one of the senses is brought into play, consider this a good thing.

The next step is to try to extend the children's attention to the sound in the following ways:

> by making the sound move away from the child's face in differing directions – immediately in front, to each side, in curved or zig-zagging lines, behind the head – but on a plane which is level with the face
>
> by moving the sound in a vertical plane in front of the child's eyes, gradually extending the movement from floor-level to very high level (by standing on a chair with arm raised)
>
> by changing the *speed* at which the moving sound passes the child or moves in the directions indicated above.
>
> by changing the dynamic – e.g. suddenly playing loud or soft or making a gradual crescendo or diminuendo

Include a commentary from time to time, saying tersely what 'he' (the maraca) is doing. Thus. 'he is coming to see you', 'he is going away', 'look, over here', 'he is going *up*', 'he is *very* quiet'. The music session affords good opportunities to use and reinforce language, and although much of the time we may suspect that the children do not fully understand our words, it is more than likely that the sense and the emotion of our language will get through to them, if only vaguely at this stage.

When the special-care children have become accustomed to following the moving sound of the maraca, explore the possibilities of briefly hiding the instrument behind a simple card screen. Make it suddenly appear over the top or round the side of the screen, as if playing the 'peek-a-boo' game which most young children enjoy. Each time the instrument appears, make it sound clearly. Extend the children's attention in this game by lengthening the distance between the children and the screen and by gradually increasing the time the maraca is out of sight. Remember that for some children, an object is conceptually non-existent when it is out of sight. They have to learn that it *does* exist in this screened situation; sounding it there will help to teach them that it exists.

A maraca can easily be made into a puppet by painting eyes, nose and a mouth on its 'face' and by adding rudimentary dress – a square of brightly coloured felt or a discarded sock with a hole to take the handle of the instrument. Some teachers might like to make an attractive puppet especially for the activities already described (something which makes sound can be attached to, or put inside the head to make it 'talk'). Having given him an interesting name, the puppet may then go to each child, touching the head or knee or arm. This is a novel way to help them become more aware of various parts of the body. Some of the children may need to be approached very tentatively in this game to avoid fear or over-excitement. Again a commentary, or perhaps a song-like motif will help, e.g.:

And he'll touch you on your head, and he'll touch you on your head,
     nose,   nose,
     knee,   knee

The puppet can also say 'hello' ♪ ♩ or 'good morning' ♩ | ♩ ♩ or the children's own names, e.g. 'Richard' ♫ or 'Adrian' ♩.♪♩ .

With children who are more mature, the touching game may be extended to include less obvious parts of the body – elbows, shoulders, wrists, foreheads, eyebrows. If the children are placed in a circle, a chorus can be improvised between each 'touching' episode, whilst the maraca or puppet describes a circle around the children (or in the middle of their circle) thus:

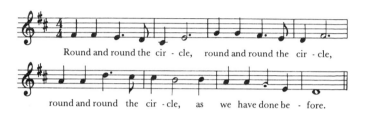

Round and round the cir - cle,   round and round the cir - cle, round and round the cir - cle,   as   we have done be - fore.

Mentally handicapped children of all ages enjoy the simple presentation of sounds which are sensitively produced by their teacher or therapist. They find it easier to relate and attend to *one instrument* rather than to an array of things which may be over-stimulating.

Choose a cymbal of good quality and with a soft beater make one quiet sound for each child, near to the ear or over the head; let the children enjoy the sensations produced especially by the vibrating lower harmonics of this instrument. For nervous children, demonstrate that this is a safe and secure experience by sometimes playing near to your own ear, or near to the ear of a colleague or classroom aide. In subsequent sessions, gradually introduce the other percussion instruments, and, if possible, a wide variety of wind and string instruments. Make the drum, tambourine, wood-block, claves, triangle or sleigh-bells say 'hello' ♪ ♩ or perhaps 'good afternoon' ♪ ♩ ♪ ♩ in the same way that the maraca/puppet 'spoke'. Be aware of the subtle differences in sound quality of the various instruments. Compare the forceful quality of the tambourine with the gentler personality of the sleigh-bells. Remember that the sound of wood-blocks and claves can penetrate very powerfully, particularly if the teacher is using a hard striker.

As a general rule, the children are more likely to respond to sounds which are made quietly, possibly because more effort is demanded of them in terms of listening. Whenever possible, encourage them to touch the instruments at an early stage. Much learning goes on through the tactile sense, and in certain instances the children's fears and anxieties can be allayed if they feel that the instrument is harmless. If melodic instruments (small glockenspiel, recorder, mouth-organ, flageolet) are used to command the attention and evoke a response, restrict the sounds at first to just one or two. Choose a falling minor third (G to E) to make the instrument 'say' hello, then echo this vocally. Some children will naturally reply to this call, perhaps by repeating the same notes.

In any group of seriously mentally handicapped children there are likely to be one or two who do not respond to the sounds produced by the percussion instruments. These children should not be regarded as non-responders until as many instruments as possible have been tried. Recently the author observed a boy who, as well as his suspected mentally handicapped condition, had been expertly assessed as 'completely deaf'. John did not show any signs whatsoever of responding to any of the percussion instruments even when they were sounded very loudly next to his ear. Later in the music session, when the accordion was being played to stimulate rhythmic responses in the other children, John began 'dancing' quite clearly with his hands. The therapist, noting this response carefully checked to make sure that it was the music and not the sight of the instrument that was causing the dancing (by stopping and starting again behind the boy). It certainly appeared that the sounds of the accordion were somehow getting through. It is possible that, for certain individuals, the extremes of the frequency band are just perceptible. For others there may be conduction of vibrations through the skin, and some may feel sympathetic vibrations in certain resonating spaces in the body.

We must also be prepared to *repeat* our efforts many times over in order to evoke responses in some children. Those who respond more readily will enjoy the repetition of our earlier activities just as those of us with advanced musical awareness enjoy hearing a symphony many times over. We shall see also at a later stage – when the children begin to enjoy simple songs and longer musical presentations – that repetition of material is equally vital.

In the activities suggested so far, we have concentrated on those which attempt to focus the children's attention intensively on sound in order to evoke responses. There is, too, a case for presenting longer and more complex material, not as a vague background, but in a situation which is perhaps less intense. We know that some mentally handicapped children who do not appear to take in the material we direct towards them have a habit of repeating fragments of that material much later in the day, or even on the way home in the coach! Our sessions might include short, complete pieces which we play expertly and also songs which we know are universally appealing. If we refer once again to our developmental knowledge, we are reminded that young infants in the home do not fully learn everything which goes on around them. There is a gradual assimilation of certain knowledge and attitudes. We can assume with some optimism that a total musical atmosphere will have a generalized effect on the infant; our handicapped children are also susceptible to such an atmosphere.

Perhaps the most useful and powerful instruments of all are our own singing voices. We have already seen how fragments and choruses of songs can be included in the activities suggested. Many teachers and therapists need to re-discover their singing voices, and it may be necessary to practise privately or even to enlist the help of a specialist teacher to learn how to 'place' the voice and to exploit its potential. Generally speaking, it is best to cultivate a quiet and intimate voice for the children we have in mind, but the possibility of variation of intensity as well as pitch should not be overlooked. On certain carefully chosen occasions it may produce surprising results to sing very loudly – or even shout – as long as this is well controlled.

Quite often, handicapped children will respond to instructions or questions when they are sung rather than spoken, thus:

Where is Jen-nie?   I see you, I see you!

Acquire a repertoire of slow, sustained melodies which may be sung or hummed to the children once their attention has been gained. Pentatonic and certain modal melodies seem to appeal to the children at an instinctive level and may have a calming and soporific effect. The slow, sustained nature of these melodies also helps to extend the children's attention and some of them will begin to feel the pulse and attempt to sway or rock to the music. Here are two examples:

The Skye boat song

Mm . . . .   *etc.*

or   Greensleeves

Mm . . . ..   *etc.*

Music to encourage an appropriate active response

When the children have progressed to the stage when they can attend to a simple musical stimulus for more than a few seconds, we can begin to encourage them to make sounds themselves, both vocally and on the percussion instruments. It is not a good idea in the early stages to simply give them an instrument and hope that they will make musical sounds; to do so is to invite breakages and chaotic noise. Apart from momentary enjoyment, the uncontrolled banging of drums and tambourines has little musical value for children.

A few of our children seem to have a naturally sensitive

approach to instruments. These children are neither too aggressive nor too timid with the instruments, and usually they try to take hold of them in a caring manner (given two useful hands). Where possible, opportunities should be given to them to hold and play the instruments; praise should always be given for efforts which are clearly musically sensitive. Generally speaking, it is necessary to hold the instruments for them at first, to demonstrate quiet and controlled beating and only then invite them to play. Encourage them to play with fingertips on the drum or tambourine, following the teacher's pattern: ♩ ♩ or ♩ or ♫ ♩. Help them to perceive the rhythmic patterns by saying 'pom, pom' or 'boom' or 'pi-pi pom' or by choosing the rhythms of real words: e.g. 'big-drum', 'lit-tle drum'. Discourage those children who try to bang the drum hard with a flat hand (move the drum out of range) and always praise those who play sensitively.

It is essential to have a variety of activities and approaches at this stage. If the children's attempts at sound making can be put into a whole musical context, so much the better. Collect rhymes and songs which have a moment which calls clearly for a rhythmic response. *Pop goes the weasel* is an excellent song or rhyme which invites a vigorous vocalized 'pop' or a hand-clap or an instrumental sound at the appropriate moment, e.g.:

> 'that's the way the money goes,
> POP goes the weasel!'

Three blind mice offers the possibility of a similar response, thus:

> 'they all ran after the farmer's wife,
> who CUT off their tails with a carving knife'

Hickory, dickory dock calls for a single, ringing sound after the words 'the clock struck One', and most children enjoy making an imaginary mouse run up and down the clock with hands and fingers moving in the air.

Mentally handicapped children especially enjoy songs and activities which include clock sounds. The wood-block can produce a very effective 'tick-tock' sound which the more able children can play with the teacher's help. *Hickory, dickory dock* may be introduced and accompanied by this wooden 'tick-tock' sound, and the chime can be played by selected children on the cymbal or chime bar. The chimes of Big Ben can be played and sung as follows:

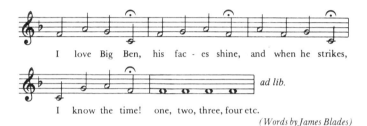

I love Big Ben, his fac - es shine, and when he strikes,

I know the time! one, two, three, four etc.

(Words by James Blades)

Although the aim here is to encourage a quite definite action, the imaginative appeal of songs is also important. In the clock songs we are helping the children to make an imaginative leap, from the musical experience of the song to the reality of what a clock actually sounds like. We shall deal later more fully with various imaginative aspects of musical activity; at this stage we are aiming for a very simple active response and we may consider the imaginative element to be of secondary importance.

Other songs with obvious rhythmic 'breaks' are:

This old man
Horsey! Horsey!
Ring o' roses
The runaway train
Let everyone clap hands like me
Down at the station, early in the morning
Old McDonald had a farm
How much is that doggie in the window?

Teachers and therapists might discover many more similar songs from all kinds of sources, and with the aid of the more able children begin to invent new songs which are based on the children's everyday experiences. Sometimes a current centre of interest – perhaps a classroom pet – can provide ideas for these songs, e.g.:

> 'two little hamsters eating their lunch,
> see how they like it, Munch, Munch, Munch'

Actions in the songs need not always have sound. Most nursery rhymes invite some kind of movement – the running mouse in *Hickory, dickory dock* or Humpty Dumpty's great fall. There are many action songs. Some of these invite finger play which is too difficult for severely handicapped children, but often these songs can involve simplified actions or may be shortened to contain just one *one* action. Thus, the first verse only of *Tommy Thumb* may be used:

In this song the children, with help, are required to find and show only their thumbs. More interest may be created by drawing (with felt pen) a face on the ball of the teacher's own thumb.

Songs which invite specific actions also help to teach the children about their bodies. Our early aims might concentrate on awareness of the face, eyes, nose and mouth, progressing later on to less obvious parts of the body, i.e. shoulders, elbows, wrists, ankles, shins, foreheads and eyebrows. This game is popular:

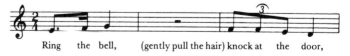

(tap the forehead) draw   the latch, (twist the nose) and walk   in!
                                      (pretend to 'walk in' the mouth)

In this the teacher or classroom helper initiates the actions firmly
enough for each child to *feel* the hair, forehead, nose and mouth.

The following tune, often sung to *We'll all clap hands together*,
lends itself to a variety of activities, the best known of which is
possibly:

> 'one finger, one thumb keep moving (3 times)
> we'll all be merry and bright!'

The most complicated version of this song has a string of
accumulated actions – one finger, one thumb, one arm, one leg,
one nod of the head, stand up, sit down, keep moving, etc.
Children who cannot manage such a long list of actions might
sing only the first verse, e.g. 'one finger, one thumb keep
moving' and then attempt additional individual verses without
trying to make it cumulative:

> 'One shake of the head keep moving' (3 times)
> we'll all be merry and bright'

or 'One beat on the drum'
or 'One scratch on the chin'

It may be necessary to sing the song quite slowly for the more
severely handicapped children.

Physical actions to songs can easily be extended into simple mime, beginning with the very obvious hand washing mime in *Here we go round the mulberry bush* ('this is the way we wash our hands'). Encourage the children to watch and copy the teacher's mime in the early stages; later on some of them will be able to initiate their own mimes and perhaps invent new ones to show hair-brushing, shoe-cleaning, car-driving and horse-riding. *Johnny get your hair cut* is another song which encourages similar mime:

John-ny get your hair cut, hair cut, hair cut,
John - ny get your hair cut just like me.
(Children's song from America)

Other verses of this song might include: 'Johnny eat your breakfast', 'Johnny put your coat on', 'Johnny get your school-bag', and 'Johnny put your tie on', or any routine activity which the children might like to mime.

Also from America, but less well known is this song which suggests similar actions and mimes:

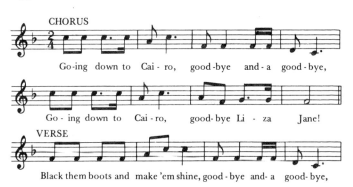

CHORUS
Go-ing down to Cai - ro, good-bye and-a good-bye,
Go - ing down to Cai - ro, good-bye Li - za Jane!

VERSE
Black them boots and make 'em shine, good - bye and-a good-bye,

Black them boots and make 'em shine, good-bye Li - za Jane.

Additional verses:

> 'Wash your face and make it clean (good-bye, etc.)',
> 'Comb your hair and make it neat',
> Brush your teeth and make them shine'.

All these songs can be effectively sung without accompaniment, indeed, if the teacher is busy demonstrating the mimes and helping those children who need physical support, she will be unable to cope with an accompanying instrument. When the songs are repeated later on, or perhaps with more able groups, a judicious guitar or dulcimer accompaniment is preferable to the piano. In the case of a pentatonic song (e.g. *Going down to Cairo*) a repetitive tonic and dominant drone is all that is needed.

In general, we need to take care that the words we use in our songs relate to the daily experiences of the children in our groups, and that they are in an appropriately contemporary style. We must accept, however, that there will be words which are unfamiliar but which must be retained to preserve the character of individual songs. Often, words need to be changed in order to relate them to everyday experiences but this should not be done to such an extent that the traditional flavour is lost.

The simple sound/response activities described earlier can be developed in such a way that the children's attention is directed towards everyday objects we wish them to become aware of. A maraca or small bell can be sounded and moved further away from the children, attracting their attention to the window, door, table, ceiling, floor, etc. The children might be encouraged or helped to point to these objects; the sound will help to focus attention on the object it moves towards. All the time, the activity should be reinforced by a verbal commentary, e.g. 'point to the window, now point to the table'. Then, the following song is introduced:

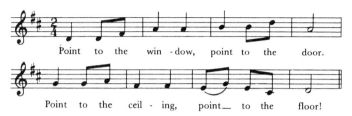

Point to the win-dow, point to the door.
Point to the ceil-ing, point to the floor!

Another simple song which motivates the children to attend to the immediate environment is *Who's that tapping at the window?*

Who's that tap-ping at the window, who's that knock-ing at the door?
(Children's song from America)

A wide variety of activities can be devised for this song. The teacher might first actually tap on the window and knock at the door of the classroom. Then, a small drum or tambourine might be offered to selected children to tap with fingertips, or 'knock' with knuckles, if possible in an appropriate rhythm (e.g.

).

Alternatively, the children might make an imaginary 'tap' or 'knock' in the air. Then, the teacher and children (if possible) will enjoy singing the following in answer:

Steph-en* tap-ping at the win-dow, Steph-en knock-ing at the door!

(* Or whichever name is chosen)

The children will also enjoy having their attention drawn to the clothes they are wearing, especially if bright or definite colours are involved. Selected children may be asked to stand up or moved to a prominent position in the group for this pentatonic song:

Mar - y wore her red dress,_ red dress,_ red dress,_

Mar - y wore her red dress,_ all day_ long.
(Children's song from America)

Additional verses might be:

Johnny wore his blue trousers,
or Alison wore her green jumper,
or Stephen wore his black shoes.

Certain children who are unable to sing may manage to make short vocal contributions to the teacher's songs. Most songs have at least one memorable short phrase which strongly invites participation; if the teacher stops singing just before this phrase, or just before the end of a song, the children may be tempted to try to sing that phrase or complete the song thus:

Baa, baa black sheep, have you any wool?
Yes sir, yes sir, — — — (three bags full)

Old McDonald had a farm provides opportunities for the children to make animal sounds:

Old McDonald had a farm, ee i, ee i, oh
With a — — here and a — — there, etc.

The Barnyard Song is also particularly enjoyed:

I had a cat and my cat pleased me, I fed my cat by
2. hen
3. cow

yon - der tree 1. Cat goes fid - dle dee fee.

FINE

to 1   to 2

2. Hen goes chim-my chuck,   chim-my chuck, 3. Cow goes moo moo,

This song is normally cumulative (e.g. Cow goes moo, moo, hen goes chimmy chuck, chimmy chuck, cat goes fiddle dee fee) but if desired, each verse can be performed quite separately.

In all our music activities with mentally handicapped children we must encourage them to make their contributions to the very best of their abilities. We should not accept indifferent or meaningless actions; it should be made clear to them when they perform inappropriately and, equally, we should express pleasure and approval when they perform well. The teacher or therapist needs to develop a quiet, intimate approach and in group activities she should try to make each child feel that he or she is quite important by being fully involved. Often, within the group situation, we need to spend time with individuals but this must be done in such a way that the rest of the group do not feel overlooked or left out. It is necessary to move frequently around the group, from child to child, adopting a position which ensures constant eye contact. Choose a low chair or kneel on the floor so that all the children can easily relate without having to turn or strain.

In all music activities with these children, it is essential to be aware of the emotional power of music, even where only one or two sounds are involved. Some sounds excite and enliven the listener, others have a calming effect; strongly rhythmic music provokes a physically active response, music which has an underlying rocking pulse tends to have a quietening effect. We must always be observant in our music sessions, carefully noting the impact of our music on the individual children in our groups and we should be ready to change our approach immediately if the children show signs of extreme excitability or boredom.

We must also be aware of the importance of the visual, tactile and kinaesthetic aspects of our activities. Children often make their initial relationships with music through one of these senses; musical instruments have enormous visual appeal and often give great pleasure to children when they touch or hold them. Movement is always involved in the production of sound; we often make unusual and interesting movements when we play or hear music. Musicians can, through their movements, impart a sense of pulse or demonstrate a rhythmic pattern, and through posture they can 'dramatize' according to the dynamics or style of the music.

The teacher or therapist should therefore make good use of exaggerated movements when playing the cymbal or chime bar (e.g. three times in the *Big Ben* song) or perhaps very delicate movements with the triangle striker when playing very soft, fairy-like sounds. The player's movements not only help to dramatize the events but also help to reinforce number concepts (e.g. if the children are helping to count the number of strokes on the cymbal or triangle). Clear movements by the player will help the children to *see* the pulse and rhythm; at the simplest level, e.g. for the POP in *Pop goes the weasel,* an exaggerated clap of the hands will show the children the point at which the important sound happens. An expansive bodily movement will highlight the sound of a cymbal brought to a crescendo and perhaps encourage the children to begin to make growing movements to further express this exciting sound.

However simple the music might be, we can be dramatically involved in its presentation and in so doing we impart the *feeling* of the music to the children. This is the beginning of imaginative activity.

Activities which evoke an imaginative response

Much of our work with mentally handicapped children is concerned with trying to make them aware of the real world, with the things which are immediately around them. Most of the songs and associated activities already suggested aim to make them aware of their own bodies, their clothing and various items in the classroom. We can, however, expect even our seriously handicapped children to come alive to less tangible phenomena. Very young babies have innate sense of fun; even dogs 'know' when we pretend to fight with them. Much of the daily dialogue in the classroom goes on between the children and their adult helpers in a good-natured 'leg-pulling' manner. Most of our early nursery songs have an element of pretence; we do not really ask 'Baa baa black sheep' if he has any wool. Indeed, most young children are not aware at first of the meaning of 'wool' and few of them will have seen a sheep at close quarters.

Most of the well-known nursery rhymes offer opportunities to pretend and imagine. The actions which very young normal children enjoy in these rhymes are so familiar that we hardly need mention them here; our 'infant stage' handicapped children equally enjoy pretending to fall like Humpty Dumpty, making hand shapes for Miss Muffet's spider, and 'pecking off noses' like the blackbird in *Sing a song of sixpence*. Teachers and therapists need to make their own collection of various rhymes and jingles which encourage action and pretence. They might consider visiting and observing in nearby nursery schools and infant classes of normal children where there is usually a fund of such rhymes and songs.

The classroom percussion instruments can be used to make evocative sounds (bells, clocks, horses, trains, etc.) and if to these are added a variety of bird whistles and instruments associated with the *Toy Symphony* we have many possibilities.

The *wood-block,* as we have already seen, can produce a realistic ticking sound, especially if it is the two-tone variety. This instrument can imitate a grandfather clock which ticks very steadily and quietly and which can have an almost hypnotic effect on its listeners. The wood-block can also make a realistic sound like horses hooves (as well as the familiar coconut shells) and to this we can add the sleigh bells which jingle like the horse's harness. Wood-block sounds are often associated with the stiff and jerky movements of a marionette or perhaps a clockwork doll. A winding-up sound can be made by scraping a guiro or razo-razo.

An effective steam-train sound can be made by striking a tambour or side-drum with a wire brush, and a three-note whistle will add to the general effect. The train sound can be incorporated into songs such as *Train is a-coming, Mary had a baby* and *Down at the station*:

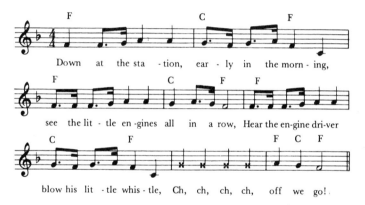

Down at the sta - tion, ear - ly in the morn - ing,

see the lit - tle en -gines all in a row, Hear the en-gine dri-ver

blow his lit - tle whis - tle, Ch, ch, ch, ch, off we go!

Musical sounds can be employed to illustrate and enrich stories, both traditional and improvised. The children enjoy very simple everyday events expressed in story form especially if the stories involve themselves as characters:

> 'One morning Stephen woke up when the alarm clock went off (triangle makes a ringing sound). He got dressed and came downstairs step by step (to a descending scale of the xylophone) and after breakfast he set off walking to school with his mummy (maraca and tambourine make walking sounds), etc.'

Perhaps the most popular traditional story enjoyed by mentally handicapped children is *The three bears.*[1] The bears may be represented by three drums – large, medium and small. Initially the teacher plays the motifs as the bears 'speak' thus:

'Who's been   sit - ting   in   my   chair?'

Later on, three selected children may play these motifs as the story proceeds.

Imaginative activity naturally involves vision and movement as well as sound. A slow, soft beat on the tambour might suggest the heavy walking steps of an elephant, and the teacher will probably wish to dramatize this by moving 'like' the animal. Some children will immediately try to do this themselves, imitating the teacher's pattern. Sounds to suggest the movements of other animals are easily made (small, scampering animals, snake-like movements, kangaroo hops, etc.) and these sounds can be accompanied by suitable movements performed by the teacher or certain children. The older children especially enjoy making snake-like movements with their arms and hands to an improvised recorder tune which has an Eastern flavour, or this:

[1] Paul Nordoff and Clive Robbins have produced an excellent musical play based on this story. See *Music Therapy in Special Education* published by Macdonald and Evans.

Small sheets of tissue paper or chiffon scarves may be dropped from a high position in the air to encourage the children to follow the floating movement with their eyes and to help them imagine falling snowflakes or leaves. These movements might be accompanied by quiet glissandi on a lyre or autoharp; selected children will enjoy either dropping the 'leaves' or making the sounds.

Visual aids, like the tissue paper and chiffon scarves, help mentally handicapped children to make the difficult transition from remembered experience to imaginative activity. Certain words may be meaningless to them, or misunderstood, so we need to introduce visual aids to try to relate words, action and imagination. Actual examples of the items we wish to refer to, or three-dimensional models, are generally preferable to drawings and pictures which are frequently ambiguous to the children, some of whom may have visual or perceptual problems. For the song *Soldier, soldier, won't you marry me?*[1] a toy soldier and real examples of the items of clothing which occur in the song will help to ensure an understanding of the words. Later on we can rely more and more on the words without the visual clues.

Old woman, old woman is a song which can be presented in this way, and simple mime can be added by the teacher or by those children who are able. The 'old woman' might have a shawl around her shoulders and hobble along with a stick; mimes can easily be devised for smoking, drinking and eating.

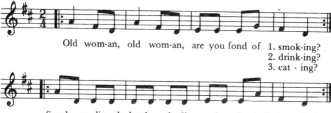

Old wom-an, old wom-an, are you fond of 1. smok-ing?
                                               2. drink-ing?
                                               3. eat - ing?

Speak a lit - tle loud- er sir, I'm. rath- er hard of hear - ing!

The last verse is traditionally:
Lawks-a-mercy on my soul, I think I now do hear you! (twice)

[1] See *The Oxford School Music Books* (Junior book 2) by R. Fiske and J. Dobbs, published by OUP.

Puppets can be used effectively to stimulate imaginative responses in the children. For some reason, puppets can command their attention and often effect a strong response; occasionally, mentally handicapped children find it easier to talk to puppet characters than to adults. Where music is concerned, glove and mouth puppets most easily enable the manipulator to play simple instruments. The puppet can 'show' the children how to play, or it may invite them to play. Teachers and therapists who have some handicraft skill might enjoy creating a variety of puppet-like characters which can be handled by the children and to which are attached bells or other items which make sounds. Action songs can be very effectively demonstrated by puppets, and the activities arising out of the songs can serve to reinforce concepts of body awareness – i.e. the puppet has a face, eyes, nose, mouth, etc. Finally, puppets may be used to enact the stories which have added sounds as we have already suggested.

Activities which add to the children's experience and knowledge

Musical experiences are in themselves educative for all children. Handicapped children especially benefit from hearing music and taking part in musical activity because they can immediately relate emotionally to the sounds. It is hardly necessary to understand how musical sounds please, excite, soothe or irritate; we know that they affect the majority of human beings (and some animals) irrespective of intellect, culture and physical disability. We know also that many mentally handicapped children respond to music which is expertly presented – they seem to recognize good quality in spite of their inability to rationalize. We must try, therefore, to give them the best possible musical experiences; these are just as valuable to them as the more obvious experiences we provide – loving human relationships, contact with natural beauty, colour, shape, form, stories and poems, warmth and nourishment. But as well as enabling them to enjoy and assimilate music for its own sake, we can take advantage of the pleasures of musical involvement to teach many things incidentally. Indeed, some music therapists base their approaches entirely on this.

It should be fairly obvious that language can be taught and extended through songs. Almost all songs contain words which are new to the children and by pleasurable presentation and repetition these new words gradually become assimilated and, later on, meaningful. Consider the verbal content of this song:

Sing a Rainbow

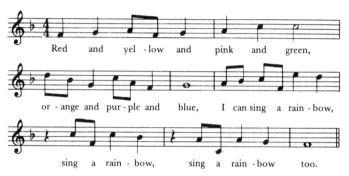

Coloured sheets of paper may be presented, identified and sorted, and a picture of a rainbow will not only reinforce knowledge of the colours but also lead on to the shape of a bow. Some children might know that a bow is also a weapon or a device to play the fiddle, whilst others might see that its shape is like a coat hanger.

The addition of new words to traditional tunes has already been suggested. The following colour song to the tune *Do you know the muffin man?* is quickly learnt:

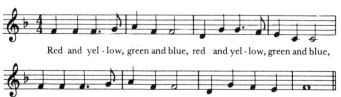

After each chorus, the children are shown one of the colours and asked to think of something which bears that colour, thus:

At first their attention may be drawn to something in the classroom, but later they might be asked to use their imagination and memory and recall an object which is commonly red, yellow, green or blue (e.g. post box, banana, grass, the sky).

We have suggested earlier how simple visual aids can be introduced to help the children discover the meaning of words. For *Baa baa black sheep* we can easily let them handle pieces of wool, either in its raw state or processed. Here we are teaching about *wool* through three of the senses.

Our simple percussion instruments afford opportunities to teach about shape, size and the materials from which they are made. Place a tambour, cymbal, triangle, tom-tom drum and wood-block in such a way that the children can easily see these instruments. Discuss the roundness of the tambour, cymbal and tom-tom, the three-sided nature of the triangle, the cylindrical shape of the wood-block. Show that the tom-tom is 'fatter' than the cymbal and ask them to say what the cymbal and triangle are made of. Let the children trace with a finger around the perimeter of the cymbal and along the sides of the triangle. If orchestral instruments can be shown and demonstrated, these also can be used to discuss shape, size and construction. The children will especially enjoy holding the instruments if they are sufficiently self-controlled.

There is much incidental learning possible whenever the children are involved either in listening to musical sounds or making them. We talk about soft and loud sounds, long and short sounds, quickly moving tunes, slow tunes, music which gets louder or softer, jolly tunes, sleepy tunes. We use words as we present or initiate our music, and we can expect that the children will gradually assimilate the meanings of these words and eventually form their own concepts which, perhaps later on, will become generalized and related to experiences other than those which are specifically musical. Musical activity is concerned with *action,* and therefore adjectives and adverbs will naturally contribute largely to our teaching vocabulary, which in turn will become more and more familiar to the children. The 'moving sounds' suggested earlier encourage the use of the words *up, down, behind, in front, around, across, on,* etc. A sounding maraca, bell or drum might move *towards* or *away from* the children, or might rest briefly *over* their heads, *beside* their chairs, *under* a table, *outside* the door. As they develop phrases and sentences they can be encouraged to say 'under the chair', or perhaps 'it's under the chair', rather than just 'chair'.

Much basic number work can be approached through musical activities. Let them help to count the instruments they see. Chime bars are excellent for counting because the children can sing as they count, e.g. C D E F G: 'one, two, three, four, five'. Many simple songs involve counting: *This old man, Ten green bottles, One man went to mow, Ten little Indians, There were ten in the bed* are all well-known examples of counting songs which can be used in their traditional forms or adapted and varied to suit the abilities of the children, or related to a current topic. For example, *Ten green bottles* might become:

There were ten white snowmen, standing
  in the snow (twice)
And if one white snowman melted in the sun
There'd be nine white snowmen, standing in the snow.

For many variations on *There were ten in the bed* see *They can make music* by Philip Bailey, published by OUP. If the teacher is able to demonstrate a violin or guitar, the children will enjoy counting the strings and tuning pegs. Selected strings of the autoharp may also be played and counted.

Chime bars, and glockenspiels and xylophones with removable bars may be used for counting, sorting and grading activities. Many children enjoy putting these bars in order; the resulting musical scales offer a sense of satisfaction which is related to the visual effect of gradation. If stringed instruments are used, the children can be taught about the thickness of the strings and how thicker strings usually make lower sounds than thinner ones.

Another educational possibility of the 'moving sound' is concerned with counting. Collect objects which roll along the ground and make interesting sounds as they move, e.g. hard plastic balls, ping-pong balls, individual sleigh bells.[1] Roll the balls or bells on the ground in front of the group and encourage them to count as each object is rolled. Arrange the objects in number patterns, then ask them to count how many are left when first one, then two are taken away. Reinforce always with *sound* by shaking or tapping the objects as they are manipulated; at a later stage, the children may be able to count the objects by sound alone, i.e. when they are rolled behind a screen or out of sight.

Pitch differences seem to be easily perceived by mentally handicapped children. They tend, however, to have great difficulty in correctly applying the words *high* and *low* to such an extent that, in the opinion of the author, it is a waste of time insisting on 'correct' verbal identification. In any case, pitch is a relative matter, and there is often some confusion in children's minds between *high* and *loud,* probably as a result of the use of volume switches on radio and TV sets. Awareness of pitch is best approached through feeling rather than intellect; it is easier to move a hand up and down to rising or falling scale than to say whether isolated sounds are 'high' or 'low'. Ascending and descending scales may be played for the children on a xylophone which is supported in a nearly vertical position to show how the smaller and (spatially) higher bars make higher sounds.

The children can enjoy learning certain elementary facts about the physical properties of sound. A guitar string can actually be seen to vibrate and they can experience the vibrations of a

[1] These bells are used by Morris dancers and are obtained from the E.F.D.S.S., Cecil Sharp House, 2 Regents Park Rd., London, N.W.1.

cymbal or a tuning fork if these instruments are sounded and touched lightly by the fingertips – or nose! If sand is sprinkled on a vibrating drum head it will be seen to 'dance' and will tend to settle in interesting patterns. It is even more fascinating to watch grains of sand collect at the nodal points (i.e. near the securing holes) of the chime bars or bars of the metallophone. Vibrations can also be clearly felt in a lightly held balloon which is near a strong sound source. All children love the 'ghost in the side drum' – it appears to play by itself when the snares are switched on and when the piano is played in the same room.

We can show the children that many everyday objects, as well as musical instruments, make interesting sounds when struck, stroked or blown in various ways. Intricate rhythms can be played on two spoons, gong-like sounds can be produced by striking pan lids and metal tubes, and every child at some stage enjoys the sound of the paper-and-comb and its more sophisticated relative – the kazoo. A cork placed inside an Ovaltine tin makes a fascinating bell-like sound if it is made to strike the lid or the bottom of the tin[1] and if the children can be shown the appropriate wrist action to cause this sound they will be involved in an excellent physical exercise. The rudimentary reed – a piece of grass stretched between the thumbs and blown and discovered at some stage by all country children – can be demonstrated and related to the bamboo reed of the clarinet and oboe, and plucked elastic bands, bottle flutes, bottle harmonicas are all well-known instruments made from everyday materials. The experience gained by exploring all these adds to a greater awareness and appreciation of the production of sound. For more ideas on these lines see *Resonant rubbish* by D. Bruner published by the English Folk Dance and Song Society (E.F.D.S.S.).

Although we cannot expect our severely mentally handicapped children to develop precise concepts of time which relates to history and distances which relate to geography, we can give them some sense of other times and places through the

---

[1] This instrument was invented by Michael Udow.

music we present. Most children watch a good deal of television which so expertly presents historical events and scenes from far away places, and these are usually accompanied by appropriate music. The children can appreciate regal and ceremonial music and associate it with kings and queens. Medieval and renaissance music, examples of which have been brilliantly recorded by David Munrow, has its own powerful quality which we associate with the past; it also has the advantage of offering short and complete pieces which some of the children can fully take in. Musical examples should be collected on cassette tape from disc recordings, radio and TV broadcasts. These might include programme signature tunes, advertising jingles, and items from the BBC 'Radio 3' late afternoon programmes for 'younger listeners'.[1] Many of these musical examples can be combined with stories, plays and pageants which involve costume, movement and scenery; in this way, the sense of time and place will be reinforced. Music which is very distinctive tends to appeal most strongly, e.g. African drumming, bagpipes, military bands, Indian and Indonesian music, flamenco, electronic music, solo folk singers, unusual instruments.

Many teachers rightly question the place of religious education in schools and where mentally handicapped children are concerned it may be necessary to examine very closely the possible dangers of presenting confusing ideas to the children. It is the author's opinion, however, that many of these children can gain a strong spiritual feeling from hymns, religious songs and sacred music. The children's own requests for the repetition of certain hymns, e.g. *Oh Jesus I have promised, Let all the world in every corner sing, He's got the whole world in his hand* suggest that they gain something more than the purely musical enjoyment from singing or hearing them. Teachers with long experience of working with mongol children will no doubt recall a number of individuals who have been especially attracted by hymns.

Apart from the associated learning which can come with musical involvement, there is much to be learned about music

---

[1] *Atarah's Music Box* is especially suitable.

itself, and mentally handicapped children can become fascinated by instruments, performers and even composers. Every opportunity should be taken to present short pieces on a variety of instruments – musicians are usually delighted to be asked to visit schools to play for handicapped children – and to relate these live performances to television programmes which many children watch avidly. Signature tunes and advertising jingles, because they are so often repeated, provide excellent opportunities to relate lessons to what is already familiar. The visiting performers will probably be very impressed by the ability of many of these children to recognize and remember their own particular musical material on subsequent occasions.

If the teacher or therapist plays an instrument well, he or she should use it at some point in every activity session. Known songs and tunes may be played for the children to enjoy, either by just listening or by contributing definite sounds and actions. Familiarity with the teacher's own instrument leads naturally to an interest in other instruments of the same family; this interest can be extended into many other aspects of musical life.

Music can open up avenues to all kinds of learning but we should beware of the temptation to use it only as a vehicle for this purpose. It is in itself a fascinating and worthwhile art to be studied and enjoyed.

Creative music activities

The creative aspect of music making has received much attention over the past decade in our schools. Largely as a result of the influence of Carl Orff, most schools have access to a wide range of percussion instruments which can be used to improvise and compose musical sounds and melodies, to explore harmony and to produce exciting rhythmic pieces and accompaniments. One great advantage of a creative approach is that it enables children to enjoy and explore music at their own individual levels. Improvisation and composition can be enjoyed both by musicians with advanced techniques and by those whose instrumental skills are limited.

It would, however, be unrealistic to suggest that our mentally handicapped children have immediate and unlimited access to creative activities. For the younger and more severely handicapped children, such activities are likely to be extremely brief and simple; much musical and social education is necessary before the older and more able children can produce 'original' musical offerings of reasonable length and consequence.

In the early stages we are concerned with awareness of, and basic response to sound but there may be brief opportunities for the special-care children to make their own original vocal contributions. It is, of course, difficult to differentiate between those undesirable vocal sounds (which are very familiar to those who work with the severely mentally handicapped) and vocal sounds which may be encouraged in order to develop positive expressiveness.

A normal baby begins exploring vocal sounds at a very early age, and when these sounds are reinforced by his parents there is an immediate increase in his awareness and a motivation to try out more and more sounds. At this fascinating stage, lengthy and sensitive conversations in 'nonsense-sound' can be observed. This activity is, however, far from nonsensical because it is the beginning of self-expression in sound – a truly musical experience.

Our developmental comparison between young normal and older sub-normal children is helpful here because it gives us ideas for things to do. Unfortunately, we can only adopt a limited number of these ideas and try to use them intensively with our handicapped children. We have to accept that there is a marked difference between normal and mentally handicapped children of the 'same' developmental age – a difference which seems to be concerned with the speed of learning and the flexibility of mental functioning.

Paul Nordoff originated an exciting technique in his therapeutic sessions involving his own vocal improvisation with piano accompaniment. One of his aims was to reinforce the vocal contributions of his child patients, with the intention of creating and extending his relationship with them. For the teacher who has to deal mostly with groups, this approach is not easy, but it does offer possibilities if he or she is aware and sensitive. Sometimes a child's sound can be echoed or imitated and later on worked into the context of a simple song or sound game.

Many songs and singing games provide opportunities for simple vocal contributions which have a creative element. The children might discover new ways of making a sound to replace (e.g.) POP in *Pop goes the weasel* or they may produce unexpected animal sounds in the *Barnyard Song* or in *Old McDonald*. They may make vocal imitations of the percussion instruments, e.g. clicking sounds for the wood-blocks or perhaps a 'boom-boom' sound for a drum or a 'bo-o-ng' sound to imitate the cymbal. The simple movements they make in action songs can be *their own,* not necessarily formal imitations of the teacher's actions. We need to be aware of all the children's contributions; sometimes they seem irrelevant at first but may in fact be very purposeful.

It should be obvious that the activities we have considered under the heading *Imaginative* are closely connected with creativity. The difference, if it exists, is concerned with responses which come from the children themselves and it is vital to be on the look out for any responses of this nature. When they occur, they should be noted, praised and developed. Mongol children are often able and prepared to contribute an action – perhaps a simple dance or a hand movement – which relates to the music we present to them.

Later on, when the children have acquired basic vocal and instrumental techniques, there is no end to the creative possibilities of music making. Many older handicapped children can invent short tunes on a keyboard or tuned percussion instrument. Some of the Orff–Schulwerk approaches which are widely used in the mainstream of music education are also useful in the special school. One particularly popular approach involves the use of a limited musical scale (e.g. a pentatonic scale C D E G A C D, etc.) which can be specially set out with chime bars or glockenspiels or xylophones. The notes of the pentatonic scale combine together very pleasantly even when played in random order, and some children soon discover that they can make simple and effective tunes on them. The teacher may wish to note down some of the children's tunes so that they can be repeated or perhaps developed by adding words, simple accompaniments or percussive effects. If he or she is unfamiliar with this particular approach, the teacher might explore for him or herself the possibility of inventing simple tunes on a limited musical scale.

Creativity in melodic terms is one possibility. The various percussion instruments can also be used to create sound-scapes. Glockenspiels may represent trickling streams or even the sun shining; drums, cymbals and maracas can create the sound of a storm. For further ideas on this particular approach see *Hearts and Hands and Voices* by the present author (published by OUP).

A few of our handicapped children can, like most normal three-year-olds, make up short songs or phrases quite spontaneously, perhaps whilst they are involved in their daily activities in and around the classroom. These songs sometimes verge on the nonsensical, but there is often a clearly identifiable phrase which can be picked up by the teacher and developed. To the tune *Little brown jug* one of the author's pupils began to sing 'Kevin Brown, you and me', which became the basis of an excellent name song in Kevin's class. Another child invented lengthy phrases about her doll, mainly to the first few notes of *Bye, baby bunting*.

Summary

So far we have tried to suggest activities which aim to help the children to become more aware of sound, to teach language, to encourage physical actions, to impart knowledge, and to stimulate imaginative and creative activity. In practice, our music sessions do not divide themselves up into these neat categories and often, we find we have many aims operating at a given time. Many teachers begin a session with the *activity* in mind, and only when work begins do they see possibilities for realizing aims other than musical enjoyment. We may of course pursue music for its own sake – this is also a valid aim.

Our music should naturally relate to other activities, and if we remember that it is experienced in all kinds of ways – not just through the ear and in the brain – we can hope to reach most of our handicapped children. For the child who has hearing problems, the visual, tactile and kinaesthetic approaches might assume greater importance. By appealing to as many of the senses as possible, we are more likely to reach a greater number of children. (See the 'ingredients' of a music session on page 4.)

For those children who are intellectually handicapped but whose senses are more or less intact, music can offer a great deal. We can optimistically expect our music activities to appeal to them totally as they do to normal young children. Music offers the possibility of communicating through the ears, eyes, skin and muscles. It is through this sensory-emotional approach that we are likely to offer the stimulation and nutrition which are necessary for growth and development.

In Section 2 of this book we shall attempt to study various elements of the music itself, for we need to understand the nature of the material we are dealing with as well as the problems and possibilities which relate to the children.

2　The nature of music

The music teacher who works with handicapped children or mentally handicapped or ill patients has much to learn about the nature and causes of handicap or illness, about child development in general, about psychology, and about music. It is in the activities in practice where this knowledge is gathered together and used, first to make and establish relationships and later to foster growth and development in a variety of directions.

In the usual course of events, musical training enables the student to improve his instrumental techniques, develop the ear, read music, learn about composition, and build up a wide repertoire and background knowledge. There is, however, a very important aspect of musicianship which is often neglected in the training process – that is, the student's understanding of the very medium with which he is so deeply involved. It is usually taken for granted that the musician understands the communicative function of his art but this understanding appears to happen mostly in eminent performers and composers.

We know that music can sometimes evoke responses in the mentally ill or handicapped when all other approaches have failed; it can create a spark of life where little life appears to exist. We can only guess *how* this happens, but we know that it does. We are therefore prompted to ask the question, 'what is music?'

There have been many attempts to define music and most definitions begin with describing the process by which it is produced, e.g. 'the art of combining sounds' or 'the sequential organization of sounds'. The process is fairly easy to describe but the affective relationship of music and man is much more difficult to understand and explain. It can, of course, be argued that it is impossible and unnecessary to capture the essential nature of music in words because music speaks its own particular language.

One particularly vexing question is that concerning the difference between sound and music, if such a difference exists. We might speak poetically about the musical sound of a babbling brook or perhaps the rhythmic crescendo of crashing waves by the seashore. It can be reasoned that these sounds are organized by Nature; they can, with difficulty, be represented in terms of pitch and rhythm. On the other hand, a composer of orchestral music can, with fair precision, employ symbolic schemes to communicate his feelings about natural phenomena through the orchestra and its conductor. Both the natural sounds and the orchestral sounds may evoke certain feelings in the listener but the quality of these feelings is rather different. The listener's emotional experience seems much more concentrated in the case of the orchestral sound. The composer, with all his skill, has within a definite period of time deliberately caused moments of tension and relaxation. It is as if he has concentrated and focused his emotional energy in a package of experience.

It is by no means certain that the ability of human babies to respond to natural, everyday sounds precedes the appreciation of 'produced' music. Common sense would lead us to assume that newly-born infants learn to respond at first to the vocal sounds (usually spoken) of their mothers; these sounds, normally presented in a situation of warmth and security, become associated with pleasure. They are perceived, along with the pleasure sensations through the ear, skin and muscles. The effect of the mother's singing voice on the child, however, tends to be quite dramatic; this is most commonly observed when she sings quietly to soothe her baby or encourage sleep. It is difficult to know whether the baby's response is 'innate' or acquired, however. Experience with severely handicapped children who have been deprived of normal motherly care suggests that there is the possibility of some kind of innate appreciation of music which is sung or played to them. It seems that some of these children do not have to be taught to make a response to music. We know that emotion can be experienced by individuals whose intellectual capacities are impaired, and it seems that music can be a powerful means of stimulating this emotion. The musician who is concerned with a therapeutic approach needs then to examine carefully the emotional energy at his or her disposal – that is to say, music.

Music can be regarded as having a number of components and an almost infinite number of possibilities of combining these components into a composed or improvised wholes. The components are commonly listed thus: *melody, rhythm, harmony* and *timbre.* Mentally handicapped or ill patients may respond to any of these component parts either singly or when they are combined together in some kind of form which may in itself have a therapeutic value. In order to understand the affective possibilities of music it is helpful to consider each of the components separately.

Timbre

Timbre (or quality of sound) tends to have an immediate impact on the listener. There are, of course, marked individual differences in 'taste' for musical sound; one person enjoys the rich, deep tones of the cello whilst another delights in the strident and penetrating sound of the oboe. The Highland bagpipe may excite or irritate. Timbre is to a large extent determined by the relative strengths of the natural harmonics which all instruments produce. Certain instruments produce strong harmonics at particular frequencies, and this may be a major factor where individual preferences are concerned. Timbre also depends on the technical skill of the performer (e.g. in the case of the oboe or bassoon which involve meticulous choice and control of reeds), upon the way the sound is initially produced (attack), and upon the nature and quality of the resounding materials from which the instrument is made. It is important for therapists to understand resonance as it is quite possible that sensations are experienced in the resonating spaces in the human body – especially the sinuses and other parts of the head – which may be an alternative means of communication for those who are deaf. We know that musical sounds can set up sympathetic vibrations in nearby objects and spaces which happen to have a tendency to vibrate at particular frequencies and amplitudes; it is likely that the human body is equally prone to this phenomenon.

In therapeutic work, we may look to our patients for signs of immediate response, either pleasurable or otherwise, to the sounds we produce. Any response may then be regarded as a sign of a possible relationship with that sound. Visual appeal, physical compatibility and certain psychological needs all play a part in the process of 'taste' but we should remember that the sound the instrument produces is all-important. In the practice of music therapy we need to be aware of the possibilities of a wide range of instruments in order to select those which appeal most strongly. Mentally ill or handicapped individuals who have marked difficulty in relating to the outside world may find unusual or exotic instruments appealing. Thus, we might consider employing the tonal possibilities of the sitar, saxophone, concertina, electronic organ, bird whistles, gongs, etc.

It should be remembered that certain timbres may stimulate undesirable responses in the mentally ill or handicapped. Hyperactive children in group therapy can soon become over-excited by some wind instruments, e.g. the clarinet and trombone, and this should be borne in mind when music sessions are planned for them. This is not to say that the therapist should always aim to provide sounds which oppose the state of the patient. It is naïve to think that the hyperactive only need soothing or that the withdrawn must always be excited. It is possible that certain disturbed individuals may need to relate initially to 'disturbing' sounds, i.e. to discover that outside themselves there exist emotional states like their own. The important point is that the therapist should be aware of the various affective possibilities of timbre; experience, and the knowledge acquired by consultation with other colleagues in the therapeutic team, will determine how music will best make its particular contribution to the progress of the pupils or patients.

In group music making with the handicapped, we have to concentrate much of our attention on the business of the selection of convenient instruments, the adaptation of them, and the exploration of short-cuts to make quick progress possible. The overall sound of the end-product is largely already determined by these factors, but there are often simple amendments which can be made to the instrumentation to produce a good sound. Often, our group efforts suffer from a preponderance of heavy percussive sound, so we may need to encourage economic drumming or perhaps experiment with various beaters and sticks. Whether we carefully pre-arrange music for our groups or produce ensembles by a 'workshop' approach, we are likely to have unusual combinations of instruments. Consider this an advantage, for these can produce dramatic and memorable music. The background music to many modern films and certain TV programmes provides good examples of the use of interesting instrumentation; the employment of percussion and electronics especially makes for new and exciting mixtures of sound.

To a musician, timbre is as important as colour is to a painter. The sounds he selects can be vivid and forceful, or subdued and retiring. Sounds may be blended, mixed, matched or contrasted. Just as the colour in a painting may immediately catch the eye, the tone colours or timbres of a musical performance call for the instant attention of the listener.

Rhythm

Rhythm is the component in music which enables the musician to work very precisely in the dimension of time. In therapy this rhythmic component is vitally important. Some theorists make a firm distinction between rhythm and pulse. Pulse may be thought of as a regularly repeated sound with or without a consistent stress on the 'first' beat of every measure. Rhythm is more concerned with temporal patterns of sound. This distinction, however, is not at all clear, and the rather academic difference need not trouble us at present.

Basically, pulse and rhythm tend to evoke a definite physical response, often in the feet and hands of the listener. Unlike the immediate response to the element of timbre, a short period of assimilation is usually necessary before rhythm is perceived and internalized by the listener. We may use strongly rhythmic music to stimulate hand clapping, foot tapping and, of course, dance. It can be argued that musical rhythm grew directly out of dance; whether music or dance came first is a moot point. At all events, with our mentally handicapped children whom we wish to develop in all kinds of ways, there is an important place for the use of music as an initiator of regular physical action. It need hardly be said that the practice and repetition of physical activity helps to develop neuro-muscular functions and, consequently, co-ordination. Young, normal children repeatedly practise physical skills with apparent enjoyment; handicapped children need encouragement to practise and repeat these skills even more. Music, with its rhythmic appeal, can provide excellent motivation for regular clapping, tapping, stepping, and swaying.

Drums transmit patterns of surging vibrations when played rhythmically. These may reach us as sounds through the air and the ears or they may also reach us through the skin. This can easily be demonstrated by holding a drum lightly so that there is palm contact with the hoop of the instrument and asking a friend to beat the drum head. We can normally feel these beats in the hands and arms (this is useful activity for deaf children). If the drum is held quite near to the abdomen we can also feel the beats in the pit of the stomach. Most people become so accustomed to this phenomenon that they cease to be consciously aware of it; children for whom it is a new experience may perceive the vibrations more strongly in the lower part of the body than in the ear – occasionally very young children are fearful of the sound of a bass drum perhaps because of this strong sensation.

The 'percussion band', which was popular in infant schools a few years ago, was a useful means of enabling children to experience the pulse of music. Modern music educators tend to decry this activity mainly on the grounds that the resultant sound is unmusical and repetitious. Pulse is probably more effectively experienced through a variety of bodily actions, especially if the legs and trunk are largely involved. Musical pulse seems to belong to the whole body; the percussion band tended to limit itself to small manual activity. Another valid criticism of 'the band' is that music tended to be used to accompany or perhaps lead the pulse beating. Externally produced music is not necessary because young children will naturally experience pulse generated from within their own bodies. Action songs and singing games allow them to choose their own speeds and to be totally involved. Likewise, good dance tunes (which tend to be repeated many times over) are soon memorized by children and thus become integrated with the steps and movement of their dances. A study of good folk dance tunes will reveal the fact that a clear pulse does not necessarily rely on a series of obviously stressed beats, e.g. ♩ ♩ ♩ ♩ | ♩ ♩ ♩ ♩ .

Dance tunes often include ornaments, especially triplets and turns, which tempt the participant to *anticipate* the so-called strong beats, e.g.

Often, when children attempt to play in ensemble, there is a strong tendency to accelerate. Over-excitement seems to be one reason for this; the pounding of the strong beats is another. Acceleration can be avoided by arranging the activity in such a way that all the children do not play all the time. Phrases should be passed from one group or individual to another, ensuring that the waiting groups relax and experience *anticipation* from time to time.

It is often helpful to relate rhythms to words and phrases; the children's own names provide excellent short rhythmic patterns which can be vocalized or repeated by clapping or by playing a simple percussion instrument. The idea of using word rhythms is far from new but has become a popular activity is recent years.

We can employ a number of approaches to encourage children to produce short rhythmic phrases:

1. By demonstration, i.e. show them exactly how to play then invite them to imitate. Remember that the visual, tactile, and kinaesthetic senses are all helpful; the children need to see, hear and feel the rhythm.

2. By first inviting them to *say* the rhythm, e.g. Mar-i-anne = ♫ ♩, then to repeat the rhythm using different vocal sounds (e.g. 'dee-dee-dum'), and finally to play the rhythm on an instrument.

3. By providing a simple tune which has a natural rhythmic break, e.g. *Let everyone clap hands like me* (see page 53).

4. By asking them to play quite freely and encouraging the repetition of any clearly recognizable fragment.

The rhythmic component of music has always been associated with the sensual aspect of human (and some animal) behaviour, and it is perhaps such an obvious component that it can become either over-used or over-looked. In therapeutic work we may wish to elicit a response which is primarily rhythmic, perhaps to enliven the children or patients. We have at our disposal the beating of drums which speak to the lower parts of the body and we have also the tempting rhythmic possibilities of dance tunes.

Melody

Melody can hardly be considered without reference to rhythm. Even in the most irregularly rhythmic tune there will be moments when we are stimulated to make movement, however small, often as a result of our anticipation of the moment *when* a sound will happen. Melody and rhythm are both important partners in dance tunes, but rhythm also has an important function in slow melodies which are not necessarily associated with dance. Rhythm not only makes a melody intelligible but also assists in taking the listener through to the end. A simple tune presented as a rhythm only, e.g. tapped out on a drum, usually has a clear shape and is often easily identifiable; try tapping out the rhythm of *Humpty Dumpty*. (This idea can be used for an enjoyable classroom guessing game.) Thus, our rhythmic and melodic presentations help the performer and listener to maintain concentration through to the end and also to derive satisfaction from the completeness of the event, i.e. the appreciation of form.

Melody is, however, also concerned with changing pitch and with very structured relationships between pitches, at least in the Western hemisphere. These relationships appear to have grown out of natural generations of the harmonic series, and can be fairly accurately pin-pointed in mathematical and scientific terms. Thus, we have predictable excursions away from, and back to a starting point – i.e. the 'home' note. Melodic progression involves varying degrees of tension and repose, and we tend to relate our own inner feelings to the intervals between the notes of a melody. An upward leaping seventh tends to evoke our own feeling of uplift; a sudden downward leap of a sixth tends to 'pull the heart-strings'. There is an interesting possibility that this empathy has a physiological basis; some people experience a definite reflex extension in the throat muscles especially as a result of hearing wide melodic intervals. The music teacher or therapist needs to be aware of the tensions, relaxations, resting and finishing points of the melodies he or she selects and uses in the day's work.

Another interesting aspect of melody is its 'catchiness'. Some tunes are recalled very quickly – even after the first hearing – whilst others need to be repeated many times before they are quite familiar. Most traditional children's songs are quickly learnt; a brief study of the melodic structure of these will tell the music teacher much about form, length and vocal range of suitable material (other than traditional) when planning programmes of work. Composers of children's music sometimes make the mistake of believing that no 'difficult' interval leaps should be included. In fact, leaps of a sixth or more add a distinction to phrases which move mainly in steps, and this distinction tends to make for easier memorization.

All young children, including those who are handicapped, need to have regular access to many melodies if their musical education is to be firmly based. By the age of three a normal infant can easily have become familiar with at least twenty melodies, mainly nursery songs, which he recognizes and is able to sing, although not entirely accurately. In school we can present a wide variety of melodies in all kinds of ways – through song, by playing them on our instruments, and by providing recorded and broadcast examples. Melodies should be presented at various times of the day as well as during the music sessions, but we need to beware of the danger of allowing any music to become merely background noise to mask other activities. We must find ways of helping our children to focus their attention on music; this attention is vital if any learning is to take place.

Melody can stimulate movement not only through its rhythm and form but also because of its rise and fall. This particular movement tends to happen in the upper part of the body – in the shoulders, arms, hands and head. Melody can be expressed in movement which involves the upper body in rising and falling, in large or small actions, and in sustained or staccato gestures. Melody can also be expressed in visual patterns, e.g. lines which follow its rise and fall.

With young or severely handicapped children, melodies are mostly appreciated for their own sake (that is, without accompaniment). A clumsy accompaniment can be distracting and may conflict with the natural harmony which is often inherent in good tunes. There are, however, some individuals who appear to have an innate sense of Western harmony. Some young children, given the opportunity to explore a keyboard instrument, immediately discover chords and make 'harmonic sense' even though they have had no apparent harmonic experience or teaching. Clearly, these children need encouragement and further opportunities to develop their special abilities.

Harmony

Some musicians find the serious study of harmony very difficult;

the reasons for this are interesting but should not concern us here. In fact, music activities which involve young children in harmonic experience are very easy. Tuned percussion instruments, particularly chime bars, enable the children to play single notes which are the roots of chords, or perhaps to play two or more notes of the appropriate chords along with their songs or simple pieces. With practice, they can develop an 'ear' for harmony surprisingly quickly. It is not beyond the ability of many severely subnormal children to follow a simple chord chart or other visual guide (e.g. a colour coded system) in order to make their valuable contributions.

As far as the children's harmonic activities are concerned, we need to retain a very simple approach, employing the use of two or three chords, i.e. tonic, dominant and sub-dominant. We should not be mistaken in thinking, however, that all the music we present to them must be so simple. In general, we enjoy material which is far more complex than that which we are able to perform. We should not limit our children's musical diet to children's songs and to music which is especially written for children. We need to look beyond *Peter and the wolf* and *Carnival of the animals*. The children hear all kinds of music in the home, especially from the TV set, and much of this is sophisticated. Present-day music is often harmonically complex and it may be the complexity which appeals to some. Adventurous harmony can give distinctiveness to simple melodies (see *Children's Playsongs* by Paul Nordoff, published by Theodore Presser Co., Pennsylvania). Teachers and therapists who have advanced keyboard skills can make excellent use of complex and dissonant harmonies in their improvisations and compositions for their children.

Form

We have considered timbre, rhythm, melody and harmony as if they were separate entities in this chapter. It is hardly necessary to make the point that in musical practice, the teacher or therapist is constantly working with more than one of the component parts. For much of the time he or she will present, and encourage the children to be involved in, songs and short pieces, sometimes stressing the rhythmic aspect, sometimes aiming for melodic or harmonic experience, or perhaps providing them with the simple enjoyment of exploring various timbres. However short these musical experiences might be, the concept of *form* tends to present itself, either consciously or otherwise.

Musical pieces, whether short and simple, or long and complex, tend to fall naturally into recognizable structures which can be basically categorized as two-fold or three-fold forms, i.e. binary or ternary. It is not necessary to analyse consciously the structure of these pieces because, in the process of their composition or evolution they tend to take on a natural shape; musical phrases tend to balance each other and there is invariably an inherent feeling of a beginning and an ending, either with or without a recognizable middle. Handicapped children often respond to music because of this orderly and satisfying form. Most of them need a secure and consistent environment in which they can develop at their own individual pace; musical involvement which includes predictable events can help them to come to terms with the uncertainty they have frequently experienced in their previous attempts at all kinds of learning.

Musical form is concerned with the organization of temporal events in such a way as to hold the attention of the listener or performer through to the end. Our daily activities should include frequent opportunities for the children to experience complete pieces which capture the attention. These pieces will be very short in the early stages and increased in length as the children develop. It is likely that this extension of concentration will transfer to other classroom activities.

Organization and evaluation

This section has attempted to analyse briefly the different components of music and to show how activities which concentrate on them especially relate to educational and therapeutic experiences with handicapped children. It is hoped that the reader will appreciate the enormous range of expressive possibilities which are at the disposal of the teacher or therapist. Much study and practical experience is necessary as a pre-requisite of successful education and therapy, and whilst objective observation is essential, it is hardly possible (or desirable?) at the present time to lay down dogmatic and clinical procedures to apply to specific individuals or groups of handicapped children.

How are we then to organize our activities and evaluate their successfulness? For most of our handicapped children, pro-gress is so slow that it is difficult to recognize; however, the first sign of success will show itself at the very outset in terms of the children's responsiveness and depth of involvement, which will be obvious if our activities are suitably focused. We have also at the outset the rather negative reassurance of knowing that, if the children were receiving no stimulation at all, they would probably regress. In the long term, i.e. over a period of two or three years, perhaps the best indication that our activities have had some effect can come from the children's parents and from other teachers, therapists and care colleagues. They will inevitably notice any marked responses and changing behaviour in both the short and long term.

In the event of poor initial response we must clearly re-appraise our material and approaches, but we should not be too easily discouraged. As we have already noted, some severely handicapped children who appear to be disinterested during music time begin to sing the songs or to re-live certain activities later in the day or even when they are travelling home.

In a stable school which includes handicapped children of all ages it should be clearly evident, by comparing the older children with the younger, that an overall music programme is having good effect. There should be signs in the senior children of an increased ability to attend and concentrate, of greater physical and emotional control, and of a wider knowledge and a keener, intelligent interest in music. There will of course be marked individual variations, perhaps even more so as the children become older, but this will be a general indication of the effectiveness of musical activity.

Fortunately, it is now recognized that the education of severely handicapped children demands teachers and therapists with the highest possible skills and expertise. Where music is concerned, the physical and emotional demands upon the teacher are especially great and there is constant demand for new and imaginative approaches if the activities are to remain stimulating and enjoyable. It is hoped that the material and suggestions offered in this book will at least provide a basis either for those who are new to this work, or for the more experienced who are searching for refreshment or reassurance.

3   Additional songs

The following additional songs have all been used successfully with mentally handicapped children. For further material the reader should explore as many sources as possible, e.g. school songbooks, musical shows, music-hall collections, campfire songbooks, etc. A useful list of simple songs and their sources is given in the appendix to *Hearts and Hands and Voices* by the present author and published by OUP.

Three crows

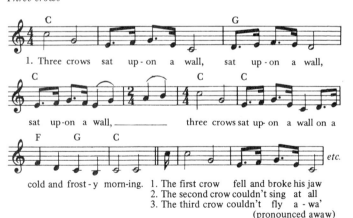

1. Three crows sat up-on a wall, sat up-on a wall, sat up-on a wall, _____ three crows sat up-on a wall on a cold and frost-y morn-ing.

1. The first crow   fell and broke his jaw
2. The second crow couldn't sing at all
3. The third crow couldn't fly a - wa'
       (pronounced awaw)

Rabbit ain't got no tail at all

1. Rab-bit ain't got no tail at all,— tail at all,— tail at all,— Rab-bit ain't got no tail at all,— just a pow-der puff!

2. Rabbit don't wear no cut-away coat (3 times)
   Just a coat of fur!

3. Rabbit don't eat no lollipops (3 times)
   Just a field of grass!

Let ev'ryone clap hands like me

Let ev'-ry one *clap hands like me——— Let ev'-ry one clap hands like me,——— Come on and join in with the game,— Re-member it's al-ways the same.———

* or stamp feet, nod heads etc.

Horsey! Horsey!

Hor - sey! Hor - sey! don't you stop, Just let your feet go clip - i - ty clop, Your tail goes swish and the wheels go round, Gid - dy - up we're home - ward bound.

Wiggley-woo

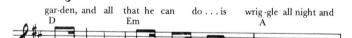

There's a worm at the bot-tom of my gar - den, and his name is Wig - gle-y Woo. There's a worm at the bot - tom of my gar-den, and all that he can do . . . is wrig-gle all night and wrig - gle all day, wig-gle, wig - gle, wig-gle he seems to say, there's a worm at the bot-tom of my gar - den, and his name is Wig-gley Woo.

Do you plant your cauliflowers?

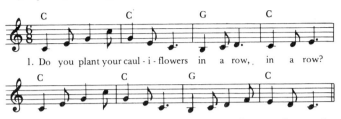

1. Do you plant your caul - i - flowers in a row, in a row?

Do you plant your caul - i - flowers in the way that we plant ours?

2. Do you plant them with your nose?   in a row . . . in the way that we
3. Do you plant them with your ears?   plant ours?
4. Do you plant them with your feet? *etc.*

If you're happy and you know it

If you're hap-py and you know it *clap your hands,   if you're

hap - py and you know it, clap your hands.   If you're

hap-py and you know it, then you real - ly want to show it, if you're

hap - py and you know it, clap your hands.

or nod your head, wave your hand, scratch your nose, say we are!

Soldier, soldier

Oh sol - dier, sol - dier, won't you mar-ry me with your mus - ket, fife and drum? Oh no, sweet maid, I can -not mar - ry thee, for I have no hat to put *(coat, gloves etc.)* on. So off she went to her grand - fa -ther's chest and got him a coat of the ve - ry, ve - ry best, She got him a coat of the ve - ry, ve - ry best and the sol - dier put it on, *(them)* Oh *(hat, pair etc.)*

To finish Oh, no sweet maid I cannot
marry thee, for I have a wife
of my own!

One man went to mow

1. One man went to mow, went to mow a mea- dow,

One man and his dog (wuff wuff) went to mow a mea-dow

VERSE 2

Two men, one man and his dog (wuff wuff) went to mow a mea-dow

Let's all sing a happy song

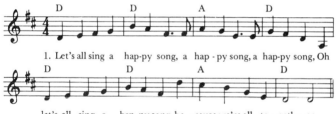

1. Let's all sing a hap-py song, a hap - py song, a hap-py song, Oh

let's all sing a hap -py song be - cause we're all to - geth - er.

2. Let's all make a happy sound . . . etc.

Wind the bobbin (The Shoemaker's song)

Wind, wind, wind the bob - bin, wind, wind,

wind, the bob-bin, pull, pull, tap, tap, tap.

A-hunting we will go

A - hunt - ing we will · go,——— a -
- hunt - ing we will go,——— we'll catch a fox and
put him in a box and ne - ver let him go!———

White stockings she wore (Camborne Hill)

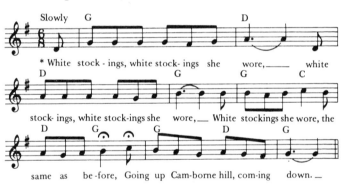

Slowly   G   D

* White stock - ings, white stock- ings she wore,——— white
stock- ings, white stock-ings she wore,—— White stockings she wore, the
same as be - fore, Going up Cam-borne hill, com-ing down. —

* or blue jumper, red ribbon *etc.*

Notes on presenting the additional songs

Three crows Although this song is better sung in the Scots dialect, it seems worth presenting in whichever style the children are most accustomed to. Most teachers will wish to encourage the children to hold up three, two, and one fingers in each verse to help with counting.

Rabbit ain't got no tail at all   A picture and some conversation about rabbits – their appearance, feeding habits, etc. – help to make this song intelligible.

Let ev'ryone clap hands like me   There is an obvious rhythmic highlight here, calling for two precise claps, stamps or other sounds. It is wise to insist on quite definite actions; some children might perform these indiscriminately if clear directions are not given.

Horsey! Horsey!   Coconut shells or wood-blocks together with sleigh-bells make evocative sounds for horses; selected children can be shown how to handle these simple instruments and the rhythm of the song should help to produce an effective walking pace. Actions to represent the tail swishing and the wheels revolving may be encouraged.

Wiggley-woo   The less able singers may be able to attempt to vocalize 'wiggle' each time it occurs. Actions involving twisting hands and arms should be encouraged, i.e. like a worm wriggling. The children might like to contribute to a large wall frieze depicting a fabulous worm-like monster. NB. These occur often in folklore – The Lambton worm, Loch Ness monster, dragons, etc.

Do you plant your cauliflowers?   This delightful French nonsense song introduces language and ideas about gardening. Some children will enjoy the jokes implied in the verses and perhaps say a loud 'no' to the questions, except at the very end when the verse might be 'do you plant them with your hands?'

If you're happy and you know it   A very popular action song which invites a precise rhythmic action.

Soldier, soldier   At first sight this song appears melodically difficult, but it is surprisingly catchy. The events lend themselves well to simple dramatization and dressing up and serve excellently as a means of focusing on the names of articles of clothing. Also, learning to dress can be encouraged as a game, perhaps more enjoyably than if presented as an occupation.

One man went to mow   This shows the simple variation of adding a dog sound at the end of each verse. Each child in turn may make the sound; this will add interest and encourage them to wait and look forward to their individual contributions.

Let's all sing a happy song   This traditional tune is very catchy and serves well to carry words which might aim to teach something definite or to provide a 'come-all-ye' chorus.

Wind the bobbin   (*Wind* with a long *i* as in find)   The actions here are more important than the words; this is excellent for chair-bound children. The traditional actions are: 1. Hands 'wound' round and round each other. 2. Make fists which pull an imaginary thread twice. 3. Fists tap each other as if hammering. As the song is repeated the speed can be varied from very slow to very fast; tell the children that when the shoemaker is tired he works slowly and when he has a lot to do he works quickly.

A-hunting we will go   Traditionally, this is danced and repeated *ad infinitum*. Teachers might enjoy devising a simple set of actions for chair-bound children. For those who are able to participate in a dance, *A-hunting we will go* seems to be easily learnt and provides a remarkably secure framework for the dance, thus:

1. Form a longways set facing partners. 2. Top couple gallop down and up the set. 3. All face front, making two 'crocodiles' which peel off, one left and the other to the right. 4. At the other end of the room the top couple make an arch for both crocodiles to go through to make a new longways set with a new top couple. 5. The dance starts again. NB Although it is helpful for the song to exactly match the sequence of the dance, it does not interfere with the overall fluency if these do not coincide exactly.

White stockings she wore   This Cornish song normally starts with the nonsense chorus 'Going up Camborne Hill, coming down (twice), The horses stood still, the wheels went around, Going up Camborne Hill coming down'. If this chorus is used, the children may make hand movements up and down as in *The Grand old Duke of York*.